QUOTES OFF
THE WALL

31 Days to Break Bad Thinking

Habits and Embrace Positivity

JONAS ROYSTER

For permissions contact:
info@paradisepublishingcompany.com

JONAS ROYSTER
30450 Haun Road #1041
Menifee, CA 92584
paradisepublishingcompany@gmail.com
www.paradisepublishingcompany.com

Printed Worldwide
First Printing 2023
First Edition 2023

ISBN: 979-8-9887279-0-3

10 9 8 7 6 5 4 3 2 1

Published by Paradise Publishing Company
Art Direction by Paradise Publishing
Copy editing & line editing by Penning For Your Thoughts

I dedicate this book to all the people I've hurt by my bad thinking habits, especially myself. From the depths of my heart, I'm sorry.

TABLE OF CONTENTS

INTRODUCTION

How much fight do you have to conquer your dream?"

-Unknown

This book is a collection of 31 quotes that have inspired, motivated, and helped change my life and philosophy.

For twenty-three years, most of my experiences came from "hood" activities or a "hood" perspective.

The Urban Dictionary definition of "hood" is successful people, classy individuals who survived the perils of inner city life. They love their hometown and desire to make it better for everyone there.

Understanding that is from which this collection was born. I desire to share what has helped shape me with everyone in my hometown and the world.

There is a quote in each chapter; underneath that quote is a suggested situation that you can apply to your life. However, you can use it whenever and however, works best for you.

Storytelling is one of the oldest forms of communication and the most effective way of remembering. That's why I decided to help reinforce these quotes with a story.

Before I began my sobriety journey four and half years ago, I would drink when triggered by anger, frustration, or disappointment.

I needed a way to redirect my routine.

Reciting a quote to myself under my breath would interrupt the habit. It helped me rethink what I was about to do.

Some months later, I found out what I was doing was training myself to change my habit loop of consuming alcohol by inserting one of these quotes after I was triggered.

The process was mind-blowing. It was the first time in over twenty years that I beat the habit of getting angered, then buying alcohol so I could forget the feeling or emotion.

For reference, a habit is something we do repetitively without conscious thought or effort. Science says that a habit is: The process in which the brain converts a sequence of actions into an automatic routine.

The root of how habits form: the brain constantly looks for ways to save effort. The loop is the repetitive cycle that keeps the pattern going. The habit loop is one big circle that I like to call the TTT. Trigger. Tradition. Treat.

MIT researchers discovered the habit loop while experimenting with rats running mazes. They found that the rats' brains generated much activity in the cerebral cortex during initial maze runs.

After navigating the mazes, they often required less activity in the cerebral cortex, even in the parts of the brain governing memory.

They've discovered that the brain converts the sequence of actions, "chunking" them to the primitive basal ganglia, reserving the cerebral cortex for higher or more intensive functions.

This mechanism operates when you arrive home and have no conscious memory of how you got there.

We all have different habits, but the loop sequence is the same. Trigger, tradition, treat. Inserting an empowering, thought-provoking quote, proverb, or saying after you are triggered, will interrupt the completion of that loop, helping form a new habit.

I ask you to keep this book close. It gives you thirty-one opportunities to create a new routine.

These quotes have helped me break decades of bad habits. Enjoy!

1

*"If you wait until you know everything,
then you will do nothing."*

-Confucius Kold

PROCRASTINATION, LAZINESS, OVER THINKING

I procrastinated on doing things differently for many years.

When I had an idea or wanted to change anything, I would tell myself that I needed to do more research on the subject. I would convince myself I needed more information before I could start.

Initially, I would be excited about the research because I love learning new things. Ninety-nine times out of a hundred that is all I would do is study.

The little voice in my head would whisper keep learning. You are only a high school graduate. You need to know more, and like most of us, I listened to that voice and kept trying to learn everything about the subject.

What it ended up becoming was a constant habit of procrastination and losing momentum.

I would study, research, google, ask others for their opinion for weeks, months, or even years, and eventually talk myself out of doing it.

Why?

Because I convinced myself that I would never be able to learn everything about the subject, I might as well move on to the next new thing, and maybe that wouldn't take as long to learn.

I knew I had to do something when this quote came to me.

I was beginning to understand changing my habits would change my results, allowing me to become successful. I needed to quit studying and start doing it.

What I implemented next was golden. I gave myself parameters for my research. I found it was the bare minimum. It was the best thing for me.

Second, I told myself I only needed to find out the information on the step I was at.

By reflecting on my many failures, I noticed how I would get caught up trying to figure out the end and not focusing on the step needed now to move forward.

The **third** was to find three successful people similar in my education level to what I was looking to do. The reason for this was to take away the excuse that my education was what was going to hold me back.

Once I did these three simple things, my problems with procrastination started to decline.

I check my list whenever I feel like I'm studying too long. If those three things are complete, and hesitation still exists, I use the springboard quote to launch myself into doing. "If you wait until you know everything, then you will do nothing."

2

Preparation + Opportunity = Luck

-Unknown

Unforeseen Circumstances, Explanation for Good Fortune, Your Haters

Preparation plus opportunity equals luck is a quote that I believe wholeheartedly. Our practice in any subject and the opportunity when it arises will create our luck.

Several years ago, I was the starting quarterback for the Paradise Hills Hustlers. My favorite play was single back wing flex close, four streaks go.

Still, every time I ran the play, I threw an interception. I started to believe that I was the unluckiest quarter-back in the league.

It wasn't until I sat down with a quarterback guru that my "luck" began to change.

In the coming weeks, he taught me to hold the football, how to release it, and what to look for in coverage before I threw the ball.

Learning the basics to complete this pass was needed for the rest of my football career.

We scored thirteen out of thirteen times for the season's final games when running that play.

A friend on the opposite team couldn't understand how I went from dud to stud overnight.

He said, "Damn, bro, you either morphed into Cam Newton, or you've been carrying around a rabbit's foot. You're just too damn lucky."

I laughed at his disbelief. "Look, my guy, you know damn well I ain't no magician, and what you're calling luck is simply my preparation for these opportunities. That's how you make your luck."

In life, nothing magically happens. There is no luck. All you have is what you create for yourself. We will make our luck through the Principle of Cause and Effect. Preparation plus Opportunity will always be the reason.

3

"Don't quit it for one funky minute. Small steps equal great distances."

-Confucius Kold

PERSPECTIVE SEEKING, SHORT SIGHTEDNESS, FAITH BUILDING

When the renowned actor and recording artist Will Smith was a child, his father owned a refrigeration company on the west side of Philadelphia.

One summer, his father decided he needed a new wall on the front side of the shop. The store front had a sixteen by a thirty-foot gaping hole at the front of the building.

The task assigned to the brothers was to rebuild the wall.

Before Will Smith and his younger brother could even begin to lay any bricks, they first had to dig a six-foot hole for the foundation.

To make matters worse, they had to mix the concrete by hand.

Day in and day out, just like clockwork, the two brothers would go to the shop, after school, on weekends and holidays. It didn't matter what day it was; they reconstructed that wall at their father's shop.

The two brothers finally laid their final brick on the five hundred and forty-eighth day of laborious work. Will Smith said he learned a valuable lesson.

"You don't try to build the biggest, baddest, greatest wall ever built. You say I'm going to lay this brick as perfectly as a brick can be laid, and there will not be one brick on the face of the earth that's going to be laid better than this brick. You do that every day, and soon you have a wall."

Every one of our steps taken in the direction of our destination is like the brick is perfectly laid. When we look up and have taken our last step, our distances will be great.

4

"The major key to your better future is you."

-Jim Rohn

Victim Mentality, Self-Doubt, Confidence Building

Try this exercise. It will require a minimum of two people and will take up to thirty seconds once the game starts.

First, you will need something to write on and something to write with, a pencil, pen, or even a marker. The last thing is you will need is a timer. It can be the one on your phone, your watch, or an outside party counting.

The objective of this game is to write your name as many times as you can within thirty seconds.

It doesn't matter how you do it or how it looks; write.

That is it. Amazingly simple, right?

Great!

Remember, you only get out of life what you put into it.

Don't let the simplicity of this game and the minute of your time you'll spend playing it have you sitting on the sideline.

If you're not willing to try it, ask yourself why.

How many times did you write your name?

The number is irrelevant.

I want to know what you were thinking while writing your name. Did your self-talk start to tell you that your writing was too messy and you needed to slow down, or how about you need to write faster so you can beat the person you are playing? What about "as long as I don't lose by too much, I'll be ok with that."

This game was a mirror of how you show up in your life. Those inner conversations we all have with ourselves are how we speak to ourselves.

Are you telling yourself you have to win or not good enough?

Rarely do we take time to reflect on these conversations, and we are dumbfounded when they show up in our lives.

The only way our life becomes the future we dream about is by making sure WE are better to ourselves.

If it's to be then, it's up to me.

5

"Don't be a professional success and a private failure."

-Inky Johnson

Work-life balance, Personal Development, Ego Checking

We have all heard stories of professionals who have checked off all the boxes in their careers, social status, and financial gains, but their private life is suffering. Most of the time, they don't notice their personal life is suffering because they are too busy building layers of superficial deceit.

Don't get me wrong, being professional and successful is what we should all strive to obtain, but that is only one side of the coin.

The other side is how we treat ourselves and others in private when the lights are not shining on us.

Just because we succeed outwardly does not mean we should fail in our personal life.

Destroying relationships with immediate family or our children. Hiding in our addictions or even avoiding a relationship with God.

An example of someone in the public eye who was successful but privately felt like he was failing himself and his wife was Grammy Award-winning gospel artist Kirk Franklin.

In 2006 Kirk Franklin went on the ever-popular Oprah Winfrey show. He admitted to her millions of viewers that he was struggling with an addiction to porn.

At the age of eight, Kirk was exposed to porn for the first time and, like a heroin addict, enjoyed that first boost to outer space.

Kirk Franklin continued this addiction for twenty-four years, and it wasn't until he wanted to align his private life to match his public success did he attempt to make a change.

One day Kirk drove from his house to throw his entire porn collection away in a dumpster.

"I tried to go to sleep that night, and it was like a drug calling me," he remembers.

"About three or four in the morning, in my flip-flops and boxers, I got in my car, drove back to that dumpster, and dug."

We have all heard of stories like Kirk Franklin's, but I request you now turn the mirror on yourself.

Does your private life match your outer success?

Maybe you're a gym rat and always receive compliments on your physique, but behind closed doors, you smoke a pack of cigarettes every other day and need an inhaler.

Or a person who gives every ounce of commitment to your church, but you neglect your obligations to your children and spouse at home.

I know none of us are perfect. Still, I firmly believe that when we can give the private areas of our life the same attention, effort, and commitment that we do to our professional and outer accomplishments, then we will start truly feeling in complete harmony with ourselves.

6

"I don't want anything easy; I want something challenging."

-Little Jonas

PERSEVERANCE, DECISION MAKING, FIGHTING COMFORT

Plato, the Greek philosopher who studied under Socrates, was taught that everything fits into three stages of life.

Everything begins at a point of energy from which it expands and grows.

Followed by a period where nothing changes, and finally, it shrinks back to its original energy point.

The first stage is growth, the second stage is stability, and the third is decay.

Plato wanted to understand more about this teaching.

He went off to the beach to ponder the philosophy. While walking along the coast, Plato picked up a beaten piece of driftwood that washed ashore and examined it.

He concluded that there are not three stages of life; there are only two.

Plato believed that everything was either growing or decaying and that there was no such thing as stability.

The piece of driftwood was undergoing a slow decay on the beach, but he could speed that up by burning it if he chose.

He could also slow down the process by protecting it from the elements.

Plato concluded that stability is only the absence of growth.

If stability is the absence of growth, so is taking the easy route.

The easy course allows us to be in a relaxed state which, according to Plato, will fall under decay.

We only grow when we challenge ourselves.

So, the next time the choice between easy and challenging emerge on the road of life, remember that if you want to grow, expand, and reach the heights of your potential, you must sprint and choose the road most challenging.

7

*"Someone's opinion of you does not have
to become your reality."*

-Les Brown

Building Self-Worth, Eliminating False Beliefs, Finding Your Identity

The grasshopper sat on the rock and watched his best friend, the ant, walk back and forth from a cookie crumb to the ant hill, which was located thirty feet from where he was sitting.

Before sunset, the ant asked his best friend.

"Grasshopper, why are you not preparing for the winter?"

"Because" the grasshopper said. "My father told me we are procrastinators by nature, and our fate is upon us."

The ant looked at his friend with sorrow and asked him another question.

"Grasshopper, do you know how to beat procrastination?"

The grasshopper shook his head no.

The ant picked up the last crumb of the cookie and put it on his back. "You beat procrastination with action."

Too many of us allow the comments, opinions, and thoughts of others to dictate how we see ourselves.

Most times, the reason why we believe those opinions of others is because we hold that person who we are listening to in high esteem. We value their knowledge, thoughts, and insights and take them as factual reality in our lives, like the grasshopper taking his father's comments for truth.

Remember, we have the power to agree or disagree with everything we hear.

Just because we hear something from a trusted source, we must first see if it will propel us in the direction toward our goals. If it doesn't, we must disregard it because it does not dictate reality.

Unless we decide it does.

8

"The year of execution starts with executing daily."

-Eric Thomas

CLARITY, COMMITMENT, HABIT BUILDING

Rob Pope, a Liverpudlian, was the first person to ever run across the United States of America four times in one year. He ran over fifteen thousand miles on his journey.

His idea of running across America was not some whimsical goal. It was an idea that developed over a long period.

"Do one thing in your life to make a difference," the words of his late mother sparked an idea that morphed into a plan.

At first, it was to cross the United States once.

It quickly shifted to multiple times when he became incredibly motivated by the desire to want to make a difference for the two charities he supported.

His objective was not just to run across America multiple times but to do the exact route the character Forrest Gump ran.

Rob Pope ended up running fifteen-thousand miles, two-thousand five-hundred times the height of Everest.

Rob Pope was on the road for four hundred days, consisting of thirty-seven and a half miles daily.

A reporter asked him, "how did you get through the dark days?"

His answer was simple "I just kept telling myself that I had to do it… I knew I had to run forty miles a day. By removing the options, it was easy."

To accomplish any goal, we first must set a clear intention on what we must do daily to achieve the remarkable feat.

Just like Robe Pope and his forty-mile-a-day objective, we, too, must find our daily objectives and execute them. Through day-to-day execution, we will eventually have conquered the goal.

9

"Move from tomorrow into right now."

-Confucius Kold

Procrastination, Doubt, Motivation

A newlywed couple bought their first home in the suburbs of Gwinnett County of Atlanta, GA.

Before the ink could dry on their contract, they discovered God had blessed them with a set of twins inside her belly.

They were excited to fill that four-bedroom home with four tiny feet.

The wife's plans to start her Jamaican restaurant were on hold until the twins had their fifth birthday.

One day at dinner, she reached for her husband's hands and looked deep into his eyes.

"Honey, once we get the kids in school, I will have more time, and I will be able to focus on starting this business. Promise."

Five bliss-fulfilled years passed, and the first day of kindergarten was upon the married couple.

The husband was not only happy that the twins were growing up

but highly excited for his wife to start her walk in the direction of her dreams.

He knew how much she had sacrificed to be an excellent mother, and now he couldn't wait to go after her dreams.

But day after day, his lovely wife became increasingly involved with the twin's activities in school.

He asked one Sunday at the breakfast table, "Hey honey, how is the restaurant formation coming along?"

She picked up the white linen they received as a wedding gift and wiped apple curry from the mouth of the twins.

"Well, honestly, I haven't gotten around to it yet." She looked away, embarrassed to meet her husband's eyes. "The twin's school needed a lead parent for their PTA, so I volunteered. But they said that position would only last till Christmas. That will be perfect timing because I will finish all that paperwork for their two-week Christmas break. Promise."

The next three months came and went, and the husband again asked his wife. "Hey, honey, how is the formation of your restaurant coming along?"

"I haven't gotten around to it yet. The twins have a Christmas recital that I am helping with, but when summer comes along, I will have all the time in the world, and I promise I will get it done then."

It was June sixth, and it was kindergarten graduation.

The twins stood in front of the school's marquee with diplomas rolled up in their cute little fists, their mother straightening their small caps and gowns while they took pictures with family and friends.

After a night of pizza, cake, and ice cream, the family watched their favorite movie, Are We There Yet?

The two parents lay in bed, exhausted but excited for what life's next chapter will bring.

Before the husband turned off his dresser lamp, he looked into his wife's eyes and smiled.

"Thank you for all that you do with the twins. You're an amazing mother." His wife rubbed her palms along his bare chest. "About your restaurant, how can I help you with that this summer?"

"Sweetie, honestly, I want to take a break if that's ok with you. With the PTA meetings, the after-school events, and the field trips, I would like us to go on a vacation this summer so I can recharge. I promise I will work on the restaurant as soon as we get back."

Life will always have another event, roadblock, or outing that can lead us away from what we say we want. If we constantly put things off until tomorrow, our today will always be the same.

10

"Reflection turns experiences into insight."

-Unknown

TEACHABLE LIFE LESSONS, DISSECTING A MISTAKE, PESSIMISM

A carpenter with years of experience was ready to retire. He told his contractor about his plans to leave the house-building business.

After thirty years, he's prepared to relax and live a comfortable retired life with his wife and family.

The contractor felt a little upset that his most experienced carpenter was leaving the profession.

He requested the carpenter to build just one more house.

The carpenter agreed with the contractor, but his heart wasn't in his work like it once was.

He resorted to substandard crafts and used second-rate materials to build his career's last house.

It was an unfortunate way to ending his life's work.

When the carpenter completed the house, the employer came to inspect the home. He looked around the house, and just before he exited, he handed the keys to the carpenter. "This is your house," he said, "my gift to you."

The house was a massive surprise to the carpenter.

Although it was supposed to be a good surprise, the carpenter wasn't feeling good because of his deep shame.

He would have done it differently if he knew he was building his own house. Now he owned a home that reminded him of his poor decision to be mediocrity.

Our attitudes and choices we make today will be our life tomorrow so take time to reflect on your experiences.

Through reflection, we can gain insight, and with applied understanding, we receive wisdom.

11

"I can do it!"

-Humanity

CONFIDENCE BUILDING, MOMENTUM, SELF-DOUBT

Two young frogs jumping through Shadow Springs Farm near Havre de Grace, Maryland, found themselves in a beautiful old barn filled with award-winning blue-bonnet cattle.

Being that the two young frogs had never seen any cattle before in their lives, they both jumped for a closer examination.

On their third leap, they misjudged their strength and landed in an oversized tin bucket with a quarter of the bucket filled with milk.

The two frogs thought nothing of it since they had jumped out of every other miscalculation on this journey. But this time was different.

The sides of the bucket were too steep, and there was no footing because that surface was liquid.

The younger of the two frogs started jumping for freedom. Still, without any solid footing to utilize the strength in the younger frog's hind legs, he gave up, stopped jumping, and, after a short while, sunk to the bottom of the tin bucket and drowned.

The second frog kept jumping, not wanting the same fate as his friend.

After every twenty leaps, he would rest for no longer than five seconds and jump again. Even though each hop seemed to reach the same height, he kept jumping.

Two hours into attempting to save his life, his persistent efforts started to pay off. He eventually churned some of the thick, rich milk into butter. Now that he had solid footing, he lept out of the bucket to leave the barn.

A powerful mindset of "I can do it" can be applied at any time, from the beginning of our journey, where fear might be at its height, to the middle, where self-doubt usually kicks in because our results do not match our expectations.

We can use it towards the end of a journey when we think we have given everything and cannot make it to the finish line.

Don't let the simplicity of this quote allow you to discard it; without the belief of "I can do it," nothing is ever accomplished.

12

"A mistake is simply another way of doing things."

-Warren Bennis

Optimism, Learning New Things, Perspective Building

Aida, an incredibly famous research scientist in Ethiopia who made several significant medical breakthroughs in horticulture, was interviewed by a newspaper reporter.

They asked her why she thought she could be much more creative than the average person. What set her apart from others?

Aida responded that, in her opinion, it all came from an experience with her mother that occurred when she was three years old.

She had been trying to remove a bottle of hibiscus juice from the refrigerator when she lost her grip on the slick bottle. It fell, spilling its contents all over the black marble floor.

When her mother came into the kitchen, instead of screaming at her, punishing her, or giving a long-drawn-out lecture, she said, "Aida, what a wonderful and brilliant mess you've made! I have rarely seen such a gigantic puddle of hibiscus juice. The damage has already been done. Would you like to get down and play in the hibiscus juice for a few minutes before we clean it up?"

Without hesitation, she did. After some time, her mother said, "You know, Aida, whenever you make a mess like this, eventually you must clean it up and restore everything to its proper order. So, how would you like to do that? We could use a cloth, mop, or a towel. Which do you prefer?" Aida's mother continued, "You know, we have a failed experiment in effectively carrying a large bottle of hibiscus juice with two tiny hands. Let us go out front and fill the bottle with water and see if you can discover a way to carry it without letting it slip through your hands."

Aida figured out that if she held the bottle by the neck of the craft near the mouth with both hands, she could carry it without slipping from her grasp. What an invaluable lesson Aida learned.

Mistakes are puzzle pieces to the bigger picture.

Mistakes are like the construction signs we see on the freeway. They are there to inform us of future potholes, past difficulties, and present maneuverings.

If we don't adhere to them when the signs occur, we will continue down the same road of destruction.

13

"Change your paradigm."

-Bob Proctor

BUILDING NEW BELIEFS, HABIT BREAKING, INTROSPECTION

While walking through Botswana jungles, a young boy stumbled across an elephant encampment. Twenty yards in front of him stood the most massive animals he'd ever seen in the jungle.

His baba told him stories, but they didn't compare to what was in front of him. These creatures were three times taller than the clay huts his baba and grandfather made back home, and their ivory tusk had more girth than him, his sister, and his brother combined.

He noticed that each elephant was only secured with a thin rope tied around one ankle.

He was amazed and wondered why the elephants did not break free, as they were undoubtedly strong enough to do so.

The young boy walked past the mammoth animals and asked the elder statesman who was bathing a newborn elephant.

"Excuse me, sir," the elder statesman put down the big bark he was using to scrub the elephant's hind legs and looked at the young boy.

"Why don't the elephants try to break free from the rope? That thin rope can't hold them if they want to leave."

The elder statesman smiled at the young boy showing off the last tooth he had left in his mouth.

"You are right young man. They can leave anytime they please, but we have conditioned them since birth that they cannot break free. Now, as adults, they think the rope can still stop them from walking, so they give up and no longer try to fight it."

A paradigm is like a program that is installed in our subconscious. It is a mental program that dictates almost all our habitual behavior.

Like the elephant, most of us operate from a program installed as a child. Now, we are conditioned to believe it is the way something is.

The funny part is we look as foolish as the adult elephant, believing that a rope tied around our ankle can stop us.

14

"An ounce of doing is worth a pound of theorizing."

-Wallace Wattles

Reluctance, Over Thinking, Procrastination

A young man was hiking through the jungles of Belize when he saw an injured crocodile.

"How does this helpless animal, one of God's longest-living animals, manage to feed itself?" He thought.

When the thought popped into his mind, a jaguar emerged through the thick brush carrying an armadillo in its mouth. It stopped next to the crocodile, ate all it could, and left whatever remained for the crocodile.

"If the Highest helps and makes sure that the crocodile can get what it needs, then he will surely help me since I am made in his likeness," the man thought.

The young man returned home, closed himself off from the world, and waited for God to help him as the crocodile did.

Hours went by nothing happened. The next night the young man prepared to eat, set his table, and waited. Again nothing happened.

By the fourth night, the young man was lying on his bed, starving, wondering why God had not provided for his child.

With the tiny bit of energy, he had left, he rolled out of his bed onto his knees and began to weep.

"Why, God, have you not provided for me, your child, like you have the crocodile?"

An angel appeared when the young man was too weak to carry on. "Young man, why did you decide to emulate the injured crocodile?" asked the angel. "Are you not as healthy as the jaguar? God has given you the same abilities to hunt, gather and break bread as the jaguar, but you must use them. You will fall victim like the crocodile when you do not, helpless and hopeless. Now get up, get your things and follow the way of the jaguar!"

15

"If you fail to plan, you plan to fail."

-Le Tyson Chatman

PREPARATION, GOAL STRUCTURE, CLARITY

Behind an old fisherman's house was a decent size pond. Every year around spring, the fisherman has his pond stocked with more fish.

Then around the fall, catching fish becomes a challenge.

This year there were three fish left in the pond. The twenty-two-pound Largemouth Bass named "Plan ahead" called a meeting with the other two fish, Think Fast and Wait and See.

Think Fast has been in the pond for two seasons but could not compare to "Plan Ahead's" ten.

Wait and See was in his first season of open pond swimming.

Plan Ahead was chilling in the reeds next to the dock when he overheard the fisherman say he would be going to cast his prize-winning net in their pond the following day.

Plan Ahead looked at Think Fast and Wait and See and grinned. "Before he returns tomorrow, I will swim downstream to the river tonight."

Think Fast shrugged his fins, "Don't worry about me, old geezer. I will think of a plan when the time comes."

Wait and See yawned at the two and said, "I have other more important things. I can't think about it right now."

The following day just like he said he would, the fisherman cast his nets across the pond.

Plan Ahead was nowhere to be found because he escaped the night before but Think Fast and Wait and See were caught by the fisherman.

Think Fast did what he had been doing his whole life and quickly decided. He promptly rolled his stomach up and pretended to be dead.

"Oh, dammit, this fish is no good!" said the fisherman, and he immediately threw Think Fast back into the pond. However, Wait and See was not so lucky. He had no plan to escape and ended up on the fisherman's plate later that night.

When you fail to plan, remember you plan to fail.

16

"Don't confuse movement with progress."

-Denzel Washington

GOAL ATTAINMENT, CLARITY, PERSPECTIVE SEEKING

One sunny Saturday afternoon, my wife and I decided to get out of our house.

We wanted quality time together away from our nine-year-old son and two-year-old daughter.

Luckily for us, my wife's mother lived less than three minutes away and was kind enough to watch her grandchildren for the next hour.

Having two young, high-spirited children in our house, merely a drive to Walmart and Starbucks has become one of our hidden fetishes.

This day as my wife approached the red light at our local Starbucks.

A Ford Explorer looked like its best days were long gone, zipped along the left side of our car, then swerved in front of us. They moved across two lanes to the right and ended up in the bike lane at the red light in front of us.

As dangerous as that stunt looked, I wasn't tripping.

That was me years ago before I was on parole, and I didn't want any police contact, but what blew my mind was their next move.

Instead of patiently waiting for the light to turn green and continue straight, the Ford Explorer made a hard right.

The Goodyear tires with minimal tread gripped the pavement tightly.

Squeals filled the air. They were so loud you would have thought they were professional drag racers.

Then as a car possessed, it made a one-hundred-and-eighty-degree turn in the middle of the street.

Now coming from our east, they raced to their green light, hoping they could make the quick right to get in front of us, still waiting at our red light.

Instead of waiting for the light to turn green, the driver of the Ford Explorer decided to make a right at the light. He drove another fifty yards to turn left into the uninhabited bank parking lot. Then proceed to make a legal U-turn in the parking lot and come back on the street. Then he could get to the stop light and make a right to get in front of all of us still waiting at our red light.

As confusing as that may sound, watching it was even more confusing.

What happened next as the Ford Explorer got to its light?

Our light turned green, and the driver had to wait for the rest of us to pass.

Sometimes, we do things believing that they will propel our goals forward.

Any movement is better than sitting still.

In all actuality, that may be the worst thing.

Movement in the wrong direction can take your valuable time.

Remember, just because you are moving does not mean you're going anywhere.

Don't confuse movement with progress.

17

"Progress equals happiness."

-Tony Robbins

GOAL MEASURING, MOMENTUM BUILDING, HAPPINESS HACKING

After being married for eight years, a couple decided that the eight-hundred-square-foot apartment in a high-rise building in the city's center would no longer accommodate their growing family.

The wife suggested they move inland to the suburbs, where the environment was more cohesive for raising a family, and her husband agreed.

Her husband only had one wish, "When we move into our dream home, sweetheart, we have to get busy fast,"

Her left eyebrow rose, and a smile the size of Texas grew across his face. "Because we need you prego in ninety days."

A smile of her own matched her husband's.

"Honey, now you know I cannot guarantee that." She inched closer to him on the bed. "That part is not up to me. It's up to God."

His right arm reached out and wrapped itself around her petite waist.

He pulled her into his chest and nestled into the crest of her neck.

She smelt the hint of his favorite Irish whiskey on his breath as he whispered into her ear.

"I know you can't guarantee that pretty face, but as long as we are making progress every night, I'm happy."

It does not matter how insignificant you may think your progress is.

Just keep going because, like the husband who wants another child, you will be happy as long as you progress toward your goal.

18

*"If you do things differently, success will
follow you like your shadow."*

-Unknown

PERSPECTIVE SHIFT, MENTAL NUDGES, ATTACKING NEW CHALLENGES

Back in the King Arthur days, there was a wretchedly poor man whose home was very bleak. It was a narrow, barren house where mice ran around and made their nest while spiders huddled in the corners and spun their webs.

No one from the nearby villages came to his house.

Why should they?

The poor man's house was in ruins.

Anyone who ever walked by his lonely home, he told of his misfortunes which he believed were his eternal destiny.

One morning the poor man sat on an oak tree stump in front of his door.

A wizard with a long white beard stretched to his thighs came from the trees.

Before the wizard could say a thing, the wretchedly poor man began complaining about his luck and poverty-laden life.

Feeling sorry for the poor man, the wizard gave him a large ceramic vase with elaborate shapes painted on the interlacing motifs and spoke.

"This vase I'm handing to you is a magical vase, and it will rescue you from your poverty-laden life.

The poor man took the vase, examined the beauty of the craftsmanship, and thought of selling it so he could spend the earnings on his usual wine.

The more he studied the beauty of the vase he knew he couldn't take it to the market and do such a thing. He took the vase inside his home, placed it on the dusty end table next to the rocking chair, and began admiring it.

"It's not right for such a beautiful thing to be empty," the poor man thought. So, he picked some wildflowers and herbs from the creek behind his home and put them into the vase. Instantly the vase became even more beautiful.

"This is still not good enough," the poor man thought again.

"How can such beauty stand next to a spider web?"

The poor man grabbed the broom from the kitchen and started cleaning his house.

Making sure to get rid of the spider webs, he poked the broom in the corners of the home and swept out the dead cockroaches and mice droppings.

He cleaned the dust from all the tables and windows and even washed the floor and the walls.

That is when it became apparent that his house wasn't lonely or run down but rather charming and cozy.

The man wasn't a poor man anymore but a hard-working homeowner with no more time for negative thoughts about his misfortune.

When you start to change things in your life, and you take a moment to reflect, you will eventually realize that success has followed you like your shadow.

19

"It's ok not to be ok, but it is NOT ok to stay that way."

-Jonas Royster

Killing off Victim Mentality, Responsibility, Accountability

The young boy was sitting at a coffee table with his mother. Only the two of them were in the house.

His father left when he was two months old, and his older sister ran away when he was five.

Now thirteen, he sat across from his mother as they ate dinner. For the past seven years, it has been the same thing every night, red kidney beans, a teacup of rice, spam, and a glass of water.

On his mother's plate, always on the left, were the red kidney beans piled an inch high and Uncle Ben's stovetop rice measuring cup size to the right.

Like clockwork, after they finished their food, his mother would uncork the two-buck chuck she bought from the corner store on her way home from work and pour glass after glass until it was gone.

"Son, things aren't ever supposed to mix with each other unless they ask, and since they can't talk, they must be separated."

After he finished his plate, like clockwork, his mother would eat her plate and then guzzle the bottle of cheap red wine she had purchased.

Then without notice, her body would start to convolute, and her once demanding voice would resemble a seven-year-old whose throwing a tantrum because she had no friends to play with.

She would place the heels of her bare feet on the edge of her chair and then bring her knees to her chest.

She'd scream from the belly of her stomach with matted hair buried between her knees.

"It's not fair, son! I did nothing to your father! It's been thirteen years, and still no word. No nothing! No child support, no birthday cards to you, no explanation! How does he or anyone else expect us to continue living like this?"

The young boy went through those events every night at the dinner table; however, that night, the sympathy that normally cloaked his heart made way for logic, and he asked his mother a simple question.

"Mom, for as long as I can remember, we play this scene out every night, and nothing changes. We eat, you cry, you get irate, and repeat the cycle the next night. I know you're hurt and brokenhearted, but how long will you stay that way?"

The young man is right.

How long do most of us choose to stay that way?

Our happiness and joy are up to us. We can either meditate on the mess or visualize the victory.

"It's ok not to be ok, but it is not ok to stay that way."

20

"Discipline is doing the things you don't want to do."

-Kabili Randle

PROCRASTINATION, LACK OF FOCUS, HABIT STACKING

Layla loved dancing. It was not just a hobby for her or a way to spend her time. From a young age, she was sure that dance was her one true love.

At her dance academy, she was one of the most talented students the academy had ever been privileged to teach. However, she still needed help to perfect her techniques.

One day, in her dance class, a new teacher appeared.

He was just as talented as her other teachers.

The difference was that while the other teachers were young, he was well over the retirement age of sixty-five.

His stringy gray hair lay along his shoulder blades while his body was as thin as a bean stock.

Layla watched him teach dance while he poured his heart into it.

He performed with grace and discipline that many younger students could not perfect.

Layla was enchanted by his hard work and decided to talk with him.

She learned that her teacher's last professional dance competition was over twenty years ago. Yet, he had stuck to his grueling training.

She asked him what drove him to work so hard.

He said, "I love dancing; however, practicing each day is not something I wake up and crave. At the impressionable age of eleven, my dance instructor mentioned that disciple is all in mind. He said that discipline is simply doing the things you don't want to do."

She stopped and thought for a moment. If discipline can drive a sixty-five-year-old man to train so hard and enjoy it, how powerful could it serve me to do the things I don't want to do even when I do not feel like doing them?

Being disciplined can set you free of limitations and separate you from the good to the masterful.

21

"Trust the journey, don't rush the journey."

-Confucius Kold

Impatience, Faith Building, Acceptance

A king of the Mali Empire once announced to his followers that anyone who wanted to stand next to him for eternity must meet him in the palace courtyard before the clouds turned pink.

As the sun vanished into the Atlantic Ocean.

Many people gathered in the palace courtyard, including soldiers, entertainers, merchants, camel drivers, and formerly enslaved people.

The king led them to a pond the size of a modern-day basketball court and said.

"Whoever will fill this pond's water in this pot and fill the dirt ditch will stand next to me for eternity. But remember, there is a hole in the pot."

Most people left without a single try. While some people tried once and said, "The king has already chosen someone else. This is a waste; let's go."

But one man kept filling the pot with pond water patiently every day.

Week after week, he served the water in the pot from the pond, and by the time he walked a quarter mile from the pond, the water poured out on the ground. Without complaint, he would turn around, walk back toward the pond, and repeat his process.

At last, one day, right before the burnt orange ball of energy set on the west side of the continent, the pond became empty. The man found a sack of gold weighing over a ton. He gathered his gather his camel and brought the gold to the king.

At this, the king said, "This gold is a reward for your patience and hard work. You are fit to stand next to me."

With understanding, the man confirmed that patience pays.

22

"All your success is on the other side of service."

-Lisa Nichols

SILENCING YOUR EGO, GREED, PERSPECTIVE

One afternoon I was pushing my grocery cart full of bags through the parking lot.

As I approached my car, I noticed that a strange man came and stood beside me as I was putting my bags into my trunk.

My nose cringed the closer he got. His once-white porcelain teeth were eroded and bartered for wooden fill-ins.

He was a body that I would shoo away without hesitation.

It was a fair assumption to say that he had no car, home, or job.

As anyone else would in my situation, I expected he would ask me for money to get another liquor bottle or another bag of dope, but he did not do that.

He only said, "Your car is very nice."

Several moments of silence lingered. I replied, "Thanks, my man, I appreciate it" then that voice in my head, the one we all hear when it's time to do the right thing spoke to me.

"*Ask him if he needs help.*" After some resistance, I did what I felt was right and asked him if he needed any help.

His response was breathtaking, and I will never forget those three simple words that left his blistered lips.

"Don't we all?"

He was more than right. It felt like God sent him there to speak to me specifically.

It was true. I needed help as well. Although I had money, a trunk full of groceries, and a place to rest my head, I recognized that I still needed help.

I reached into my back pocket, pulled out my wallet, and gave him more than enough money for food and shelter for a couple of days.

It became clear to me that no matter how much money, achievements, or luxury we have, we all need help.

The flip side is that no matter how much money you lack or how many problems you may have, you still have an opportunity to help others by simply giving.

Even if it is only a few kind words, you can provide that freedom, which can be priceless for the other person.

Maybe that man was just a homeless stranger, but to me, he was more than that. He was sent by the Highest Loving Power to open my eyes. To show me that there is one thing, among all other values and achievements, which is very important and irreplaceable for each person.

It is a true gift, and it is called Giving.

23

"Perseverance is a great substitute for talent."

-Steve Martin

Resilience, Self-Doubt, Weariness

In the backcountry of Texarkana, Arkansas, there was a significantly older man everyone in town knew and respected because his skill with an ax was remarkable.

The older man was responsible for erecting ninety-five percent of the town's government buildings, bridges, and dams.

Everyone was devastated when he passed away on the eve of the town's inaugural parade to celebrate his contributions.

In his will, he left all that he owned to his surviving three children, Jack, Melissa, and Harry.

Jack, the oldest, left the log cabin his father built at the turn of the century. Melissa, the middle child, was left with the cow, the chicken, and the farm.

In contrast, the youngest of the three, Harry, was left with a pair of well-used cowhide gloves and his father's trusty ol' axe passed down through the generations.

Jack was only married six months before his father passed and was grateful that his father had the foresight to leave the cabin he had built by hand.

Jack and his family settled in with ease.

Melissa, who left the cow, the chicken, and the farm, eventually dropped out of college. She couldn't handle the upkeep of the land and animals.

Melissa started trading milk at the farmer's market in their little town to keep the money coming in.

Harry, the youngest who was left with his father's cow hides, gloves, and axe, started earning his bread and butter by utilizing all that had been given to him.

Many years passed. The cabin left to Jack looked about as out of shape as Jack himself.

Melissa's cow on the farm was almost as lazy as she was now.

On the other hand, Harry hadn't stopped working for a minute.

He, like his father, helped erect more buildings in the middle of town, construct bridges, build dams, and raise mills. Harry earned money and bought his cabin, land, and a cow.

One night at dinner, Melissa was visiting her older brother Jack, and they could not believe how Harry had done so well with himself.

He was the youngest, and that wasn't supposed to happen, so the two of them conspired to steal Harry's axe and gloves because they believed something magical about them.

Once they were in their possession, they tried working with it, but it didn't seem to do much.

Apparently, by putting gloves on and holding the axe, they thought the skill would magically be bestowed on them. Once again, they were wrong.

After a long day at Octoberfest, Harry returned home and noticed his gloves and axe were missing.

He didn't panic for one second because perseverance taught him one major lesson in life. Never confuse a single defeat with a final defeat.

Harry knew his accomplishments were built by persevering while attaining the skill to use the gloves and axe, not from the gloves and axe themselves.

He was a skilled man.

24

"Don't say I can't; say how can I?"

-Jim Kwik

CONFUSION, OVERWHELMED, CREATIVITY

A young boy born without a left arm was sent to Jiu-Jitsu lessons. His mother thought it would help with his confidence.

He began taking classes with a very old Japanese master, and the master taught the boy the same takedown in every session.

On occasion, the one-armed boy would witness other students learning different techniques after different techniques.

One night after practice, he asked the master why wasn't he learning anything else. Was he not good enough?

The master kneeled, tightened the young boy's white belt, and searched into his eyes.

"Don't worry about anyone else. Just focus on this one move."

Nine months into the boy's training, there was colossal tournament three states away, and the old master entered the young boy. Terrified couldn't explain how the young boy felt.

"I can't win. I only know one move." The young boy was ranked sixteenth out of sixteen participants when the tournament began.

Still, to his surprise, when the first match began, he countered and quickly grabbed his opponent – and to the shock of the spectators – promptly took down his opponent and made him submit.

Instant win!

The second match was a little more complicated than the first because he was no longer a surprise to his opponents; however, three minutes into the game, his second opponent suffered the same fate as his first by pulling off the same technique.

By the third match, the young boy's confidence grew, and the spectators could tell the difference within minutes.

The young boy won his third match and found himself in the finals facing a much bigger, stronger, and more formidable opponent who had won this tournament four years standing.

At first, the young boy was overmatched. He was agile enough not to fall victim to the more prominent opponent's grappling; however, going into the final five-minute round, he was down by three points.

Before the last game started, the referee and the tournament organizers pulled the master to the side. They asked if he wanted to withdraw the student. "No, he will fight."

The crowd was on the edge of their seat as the final round began. The opponent stepped and grabbed the young one-armed boy and pulled him towards him.

For a second, it looked as if it was all over.

But then the one-armed boy reached with his right hand, grabbed his opponent's uniform, fell to the ground, and arm-barred his opponent into submission to win the match!

The crowd went nuts.

Out of sixteen participants, the one-armed boy was the tournament champion in his division.

On the drive home, the young boy asked his teacher, "Was this a set-up? Did they just let me win because I only have one arm? I only know one technique. These guys know hundreds. I can't possibly be this good!"

The teacher replied, "No, you won fair and square. There are two reasons why you won. First, because you mastered one of the most devastating techniques in Jiu- Jitsu. And the only known way to defend against that technique is to grab the left arm."

What appeared to be an incredible weakness – was, in fact, his greatest strength.

25

"Hard work beats talent when talent doesn't work hard."

-Mike Ditka

Practicing, Comparison, Endurance

Once, a young boy was the fourth of five kids born. His mother was a bank teller, and his father was an equipment manager.

Due to the dangers of living in Brooklyn, his parents decided to move to the slower pace of living in Wilmington, North Carolina.

At a very young age, the boy's relationship with his father was a critical factor in his ultra-competitiveness, and their mutual love for sports was the root of their relationship.

Wanting to be like his older brother, he tried out for the basketball team during his sophomore year of high school.

To his coach's credit, the boy didn't fit the mold of a typical shooting guard.

His height was a factor, and he had to fix his shot.

Without much hesitation, the high school coach did what all men who wanted to keep their job for another year did. He picked the taller, more developed kid instead.

The young boy, who was competitive at everything he set forth to do, did not take the rejection kindly and was determined to make it on the team at next year's tryouts. He planned to practice.

His mission was to build the skill; to do that, he knew he had to work harder than the guys with the talent.

Every day he got to school before everyone else and spent his mornings in the gym.

He was determined to become the best basketball player.

Most mornings, the other physical education teachers had to drag him out of the gym so he would not miss the first period.

That following season a spot on the varsity team opened, and the young boy tried his luck.

Not to his surprise, he made the team; however, the coach still didn't see the top-tier talent he thought he was showing in practices.

This led the coach to keep him on the bench most nights so he could hand out water bottles and towels to his tired teammates.

He did not falter or quit the team. He did the only thing he knew how to do, and that was to double down on what got him on the team in the first place, and that was practice.

Eventually, the young man got more playing time and, by his senior year, was awarded a scholarship to the University of North Carolina at Chapel Hill.

He was the number three pick in the 1984 draft.

He eventually became the basketball icon Michael Jordan.

Michael Jeffrey Jordan is the epitome of how hard work beats talent when talent doesn't work hard.

26

"No reason for plan B because it distracts from plan A."

-Will Smith

INDECISIVENESS, FOCUS, CLARITY

Bernard took the same route home from school on Monday through Friday without skipping a beat.

A Taekwondo studio was in the middle of his route home in a run-down strip mall.

Each day on his way home, Bernard would stop outside the oversized window and be in awe of the vibrance of activity.

The students, who were frail and skinny like he was, were breaking boards with their fists, doing spinning heel kicks in mid-air reminded him of the Jackie Chang movies.

Often, there would be days when Bernard would be in a trance outside the dojo for hours, mimicking all the movements he watched.

On the last day of school, before the summer let out, he went to stand in front of the window, but this time the sensei was outside waiting for him as he arrived.

"Son, I see you faithfully every day outside the widow, watching and even practicing some of the moves you see my students doing. Why have you not asked your parents to enroll you?"

"Because, sir, I not only watch just your students, I go down the street and watch the boxers at the boxing gym spar, and I do the same thing there. I watch and learn from that window. I will be a decent fighter one day if I do both of these things well. What do you think of this idea?"

The sensei focused on the peach fuzz below Bernard's nose and spoke.

"The man who chases two rabbits catches neither one."

In the book the Power of Awareness by Neville Goddard, he harped on this fact repeatedly in chapter six, titled Attention.

James 1:8 states, "A double-minded man is unstable in all his ways."

Suppose our attention is on anything other than our genuine desire, our plan A. We will then be distracted by chasing two rabbits in that case.

27

"Everything is hard before it is easy."

-Geothe J.W.

PERSISTENCE, PERSPECTIVE, PERFORMANCE

One Sunday morning, a pastor's daughter broke into a rant.

She was complaining to her father that her life was pathetic and that she didn't know how she would make it.

She was fed up with being fed up and was tired of struggling all the time. It seemed like one problem was solved, and another soon followed.

Her father, a chef by profession, took her to the kitchen. He filled three pots with water and placed each burner on a high fire.

As each bank began to boil, he identified three yams in one pot, two large brown eggs in the second pot, and a ground cup of Uganda's Good African coffee beans and placed it in the third pot.

He then let them sit and boil without saying a word to his daughter. The daughter sighed and anxiously waited, wondering what he was doing.

After twenty-five minutes, one after another, he turned off all three burners.

He took the yams out of the pot and placed them in a bowl. Next, he took the oversized plastic spoon, pulled the boiled eggs out of the pot, and put them in a bowl. He then ladled the coffee out and placed it in a cup.

He asked when he turned to his daughter, whose arms were folded across her chest. "Sweetheart, what do you see?"

"Yams, eggs, and coffee," she replied under her breath.

"Sweetheart, I advise you to take a closer look and touch the yams.'" She unfolded her arms, reached out to touch both yams, and pointed out that they were soft.

He then asked her to take an egg and break it. After tapping the egg on the counter, she pulled off the shell and witnessed the hard-boiled egg. Finally, he asked her to sip the coffee. Its rich aroma brought a smile to her face.

"Dad, what does this mean?"

Her father tapped his hand on the two bar stools next to the island and gestured for them to have a seat.

He then explained to his daughter that the yams, the eggs, and the coffee beans had each faced the same struggle, the same adversity– the boiling water. However, each one responded differently.

The yams went in strong, hard, and unrelenting, but they became soft and weak in boiling water.

The eggs were fragile, with the thin outer shell protecting their liquid interior until it was put in the boiling water. Then the inside of the egg became hard.

However, the ground coffee beans were unique. After being exposed to boiling water, they changed it and created something new.

Meeting his daughter's almond shape eyes with his, he asked,

"Which are you, sweetheart? When struggle and adversity knock on your door, how do you respond? Are you a yam, an egg, or a coffee bean?"

28

"Commitment is staying true to what you said you were to do long after the mood you said it in has left."

-Inky Johnson

SHINY OBJECT SYNDROME, LACK OF COMMITMENT, INTEGRITY

A group of friends who met in college had a tradition of mountain climbing at least once a year.

After college, they all went their own way; however, this tradition was their excuse to stay connected and share what was going on in their lives.

So, this year, the group of friends decided to go to Tanzania near the Kenya border to climb Mount Kilimanjaro's tallest free-standing mountain.

Mount Kilimanjaro has three summits, with the most famous being Kibo which stands at nineteen thousand three hundred and forty-one feet and can be viewed from countless viewpoints for the less experienced climbers.

In contrast, daring and experienced climbers who want a challenge would reach Uhuru Peak.

As the group of friends was climbing to the top, they realized the climb was more challenging than expected and would be best to stop at the last possible campsite.

While setting up camp, Trayvon noticed other hikers climbing past them.

He thought to himself, why not continue to the top? They've made it this far. He asked if any of his friends wanted to join him to complete the hike, but no one was willing to because of the dangers of the high altitude.

They were satisfied with where they were. Trayvon wanted to climb to the top however was experienced enough to know not to go alone on such a dangerous ascent.

Luckily for him, a group of experienced climbers they had seen a couple of days before was walking past their camp on the way to the top.

Trayvon saw the opportunity and asked if they could join their group, and they gladly accepted him.

When they finally reached the top, there were a handful of people already there who welcomed Trayvon and the new group with a round of applause.

Trayvon was surprised about the final climb; it was not as difficult as so many others had told him.

Suddenly a man stepped next to Trayvon, introduced himself, and started a conversation.

After a few moments, Trayvon shared with the man his thoughts about the climb's difficulty and how he was surprised that there were only a handful of people there.

"Why aren't there more people at the top? It's gorgeous up here and not hard to climb, even with the elevation?"

The veteran climber smiled, "You see those people there," and pointed his finger at where Trayvon, his friends, and many others had set their camps.

"Most people in the crowd are happy with what they find easy. They never think that they have the potential to achieve more," the veteran climber continued, "Even people who are not happy. They don't want to take any risks. Many do not show courage and remain part of the crowd their whole life. The worst part is that they also keep complaining about the handful of people who dare to do something different."

After hearing that, Trayvon started asking himself how many times he had been like that.

He promised himself that he would never act like that again.

From then on, he was always determined to find the courage to remain committed to finishing what he set out to do regardless if the mood he said it in had vanished.

29

"Impossible is not a fact. It's an opinion."

-Tony Robbins

Not Listening to Other People's Opinions, Optimism, Solution Seeking

At the innocent age of seven, Emilio's mother, the Academy Director at a prestigious private school in the uber-rich zip code of La Jolla, California, died while on her way to work from what doctors called a brain aneurysm.

Emilio's father, a horse trainer by trade, was now at the helm of the household, trying to maintain a lifestyle on only one income.

Even after acquiring two more jobs, Emilio's father couldn't keep up. He eventually lost everything he and his late wife built together.

From eight years of age to his senior year in high school, Emilio's father moved the two of them three times a year, every year, looking for a better opportunity to train horses.

They moved from stable to stable, ranch to ranch, training horses.

Emilio's education was constantly interrupted. To this day, I still don't know if Emilio was able to retain any information from school with all the moving, he and his father did.

For his Senior class project, the students were tasked to write a detailed plan outlining what the next ten years looked like after graduating high school.

Emilio did not hesitate for one second and wrote an eleven-and-a-half-page paper about his aim to be a world-renowned horse breeder, trainer, and equestrian.

Emilio's paper was full of details of who he was doing this for, why he was doing this, and how he would accomplish this feat.

He even drew a location of the buildings, stables, and a detailed house plan.

Two days later, he received his paper back with a big red F on the cover page.

When the bell rang for class to end, Emilio walked to the desk where his teacher was sitting. Trying to find his voice buried underneath his disappointment, he asked, "Why did I receive an F? Half the class gave you a one-page paper, and no one gave you a detailed plan as requested."

His English teacher took her pointer finger, pushed her square-framed reading glasses higher onto the bridge of her nose, and responded.

"Emilio, this dream is so unrealistic for a boy like you. Look at you. Your family has no money, you have zero resources, and you don't know a thing about horses. You must be wealthy to own horses. There is no way on God's green earth that you will ever accomplish this."

Emilio stuffed his paper back into his backpack.

"Emilio, if you want a passing grade on the final project, rewrite your paper with some realistic goals.

When Emilio arrived home, he spoke with his father immediately, who was in their living room apartment ironing.

Emilio sat on the rocking chair his late mother used to rock him in. He told his father about his conversation with his teacher.

Emilio's father turned the T.V. off and looked Emilio square in his eyes.

"Mijo, this decision is yours and only yours to make. Remember, whatever you do will determine the rest of your life."

After several days, Emilio stood again in front of his teacher's desk after class.

She smiled as he reached into his backpack. The paper he gently placed on the stack of papers she was grading wiped the smile from her lips.

The paper was the same as she had given him several days ago.

Emilio looked his teacher square in her eyes like his father had done him several days earlier, tilted his shoulders back, and spoke with conviction.

"Nothing is impossible. You can keep your F, and I will keep my dream."

Now Emilio Perez owns a four-thousand-square-foot house in the middle of a two-hundred-acre horse ranch, and he still has that school paper, which is now framed over the fireplace.

30

"How you do anything is how you do everything."

-Jim Kwik

Mediocrity Mindset, Standard Setting, Professionalism

Doctor Malik Tyler was fighting for his patient's life.

Little Imani had a rare disease and urgently needed a blood transfusion to survive.

The only hope for the six-year-old was to receive a blood donation from her twin brother, not only because the siblings had the same blood type but also because he had survived her condition.

His blood, therefore, contained an antibody that could save Imani's life.

When Dr. Malik asked the boy if he would agree to give blood to his sister, the youngster was initially hesitant. But when the physician explained that it was the only way to save his sister's life, he agreed.

The boy's parents took him to the hospital, where he was put on a gurney beside his twin.

Both were hooked up to IV's. The transfusion proceeded as the boy's blood left his body and entered his sister's.

As the two siblings lay next to each other during the treatment, the doctor was relieved as he saw color return to Imani's face.

But the heroic young boy suddenly became very serious when the procedure was finished. He asked the doctor, "How soon until I start to die?"

Dr. Malik stared into the brothers pebble brown eyes and saw the terror hiding behind his display of heroism. He took the brother's fist into his hands and unballed them. "Young man, you saving your sister's life does not mean you had to give up yours."

A smile from ear to ear spread across the young brother's face. The little boy had thought that he would be giving his life to save his sister with his blood donation. Those in the room were stunned at the immensity of the boy's willingness.

He was ready to give his life to another. How we do anything predicates how we do everything.

FINAL WORDS

These quotes are the gaslight to the fire of my change, and I hope they will do the same for you.

Remember, none of us are perfect, so don't tear yourself apart when you make a human mistake.

Just locate the quote in the book that best fits the situation.

Wipe the dirt off your clothes, then the blood from your scrapes, get on up, and get after it!

Because sitting on our butt, wallowing around in our mess, will get us nowhere.

We must take aggressive steps to walk up the staircase to our greatness.

Until we talk again, my friends, let's keep growing.

Our greatness depends on it.

Also, if you have quotes that you use in your life already, please share them with me.

Tag me. @jonasroyster and use the hashtag #qotw.

I would love to hear them.

www.ingramcontent.com/pod-product-compliance
Lightning Source LLC
Chambersburg PA
CBHW060528130626
46553CB00002B/687

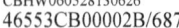